PEANUT AND OTHER FOOD ALLERGIES

Caitie McAneney

New York

Published in 2015 by The Rosen Publishing Group, Inc.
29 East 21st Street, New York, NY 10010

First Edition

Editor: Caitie McAneney
Book Design: Mickey Harmon

Photo Credits: Cover (series logo) Alhovik/Shutterstock.com; cover (banner) moham'ed/Shutterstock.com; cover (girl) Valua Vitaly/Shutterstock.com; cover (peanut products) tomsza/Shutterstock.com; p. 5 Jamie Wilson/Shutterstock.com; p. 7 Image Point Fr/Shutterstock.com; p. 9 gorillaimages/Shutterstock.com; p. 11 Chubykin Arkady/Shutterstock.com; p. 12 Jiri Hera/Shutterstock.com; p. 13 (peanuts) Sergio33/Shutterstock.com; p. 13 (walnuts) Pincarel/Shutterstock.com; p. 13 (cashews) mayakova/Shutterstock.com; p. 14 Valentyn Volkov/Shutterstock.com; p. 15 Linda Hughes/Shutterstock.com; p. 17 KPG Payless2/Shutterstock.com; p. 19 Peter Dazeley/The Image Bank/Getty Images; p. 21 Ron Levine/Digital Vision/Getty Images.com; p. 22 Pressmaster/Shutterstock.com.

McAneney, Caitlin.
Peanut and other food allergies / Caitie McAneney.
    pages cm. — (Let's talk about it)
Includes bibliographical references and index.
ISBN 978-1-4777-5807-6 (pbk.)
ISBN 978-1-4777-5808-3 (6 pack)
ISBN 978-1-4777-5809-0 (library binding)
1. Food allergy—Juvenile literature. 2. Peanuts—Juvenile literature. I. Title.
RC596.M38 2015
616.97'5—dc23
                        2014024180

Manufactured in the United States of America

CPSIA Compliance Information: Batch #CW15PK: For Further Information contact Rosen Publishing, New York, New York at 1-800-237-9932

CONTENTS

WHAT ARE ALLERGIES?

Do you have a food allergy? Maybe you have a friend or family member who does. Having a food allergy might make you feel left out. You might wonder why you can't eat the foods other people eat.

An allergy is the way your immune system **reacts** to a certain food, animal, or plant. Your immune system is your body's **protection** against sickness. But sometimes it makes a mistake and thinks something that's safe is harmful. When your immune system fights the **allergen**, you feel sick.

Allergies often run in families. If your parent is allergic to nuts, you might also be allergic to nuts.

Your immune system is your body's fighter. It fights the germs that cause illnesses. It battles allergens by making **histamine** in your body. Histamine makes you feel sick.

KINDS OF ALLERGIES

Some people have seasonal allergies. That means they're allergic to something in their surroundings during certain seasons. Many people are allergic to pollen from flowers, weeds, and trees in the spring. Other people are allergic to dust or mold.

Do you sneeze every time you pet a dog or cat? Some people are allergic to animals. Others are allergic to bug bites, such as bee stings. Some of the hardest allergies to deal with are food allergies. Food allergies are bad reactions to eating certain types of food.

Seasonal allergies can be treated with certain medicines, or drugs. But if you have a food allergy, you have to stay away from that food altogether.

COMMON FOOD ALLERGENS

SIGNS OF AN ALLERGY

How do you know if you're allergic to something? Your body gives you certain signs, called symptoms, that let you know you're having an allergic reaction. Some food allergies might give you itchy eyes and a runny nose. You may wheeze, or breathe loudly. You may get hives, which makes your skin red and itchy.

Some people have small reactions that go away quickly. Other people have **severe** reactions. They might have trouble breathing, and their lips and tongue might swell.

TELL ME MORE

Food allergies can cause an upset stomach. You might even throw up or have to use the bathroom.

If you have allergy symptoms, go to a doctor. They can find out what you're allergic to by doing a simple test on your skin.

FOOD ALLERGIES

It's important that everyone is educated about food allergies. That's because, unlike seasonal or pet allergies, food allergies are an everyday danger. An allergic person has to keep away from the food at all times.

There are eight major food allergens. Those are peanuts, tree nuts, eggs, milk, soy, wheat, fish, and shellfish. People who are allergic need to make sure they don't eat these foods by mistake. They also need to make sure they don't eat food that has touched the allergen.

People with food allergies sometimes can't eat at places that make their food near certain allergens, such as peanuts or wheat.

TELL ME MORE

People around an allergic person need to be willing to keep allergens away, too. If your classmate is allergic to peanut butter, avoid eating it near them.

11

GOING NUTS OVER PEANUTS

Peanuts are one of the most common food allergens. People with peanut allergies can't eat peanut butter or anything that contains peanuts, such as some cookies or sauces.

Peanuts aren't nuts at all. They're legumes, or plants that have bean pods, such as peas and green beans.

When someone who's allergic to peanuts eats one, their body thinks it's an enemy. It sends histamine to fight the allergen. This can make a person feel faint or dizzy. They could have a stomachache, hives, itchy eyes, a bad cough, or a tight throat. Peanut allergies are very serious because severe reactions can make it hard to breathe.

WALNUTS

PEANUTS

CASHEWS

TELL ME MORE

Some people are very allergic to tree nuts, such as walnuts, pecans, pistachios, and cashews. These allergies are very serious, too.

13

EVERYDAY FOOD

People can also be allergic to foods that are part of our everyday meals, such as eggs and milk. Egg allergies happen mostly in kids under age five. Luckily, most kids outgrow this allergy. There are eggs in baked goods and other prepared dishes.

Some people can't have milk products because they're **lactose intolerant**, but having a milk allergy is different. People who are lactose intolerant may have bad stomachaches, but people with milk allergies can have an allergic reaction, such as trouble breathing.

Many people are also allergic to fish, such as tuna, or shellfish, such as shrimp and clams. These people need to be very careful in seafood restaurants.

SOY AND WHEAT

People who are allergic to milk can drink soymilk instead, unless they're allergic to soy! Soy comes from soybeans, which are legumes like peanuts. Soy is found in many baked goods and Asian dishes.

Wheat allergies are **challenging** to deal with because wheat is used in bread, cereal, pasta, crackers, chocolate, and baked goods. Some people can't eat wheat because they have celiac disease. This disease means they can't eat gluten, which is found in wheat. But celiac disease and wheat allergies are very different.

If you get sick when you eat wheat, go to your doctor. They'll be able to tell you if you have a wheat allergy or celiac disease.

If you have a wheat allergy, you need to learn which foods are safe and which are not. For example, you can eat rice, but not pasta.

17

SPEAK UP AND STAY SAFE!

How can you avoid eating foods you're allergic to? First, learn more about what foods you can eat. You and your parents should read food labels. If you're allergic to soy, avoid anything that says "soy" on the label.

It's important to speak up about your allergy. Tell your teachers, friends, family members, and anyone who is making you food. They'll be more careful while cooking. At school, your teacher will probably have you sit at an allergen-free lunch table and learn in an allergen-free classroom.

You should tell people at restaurants about your allergy. They'll make sure that the allergen isn't put in your food.

A food label may say that the food was made in a place that also makes foods containing allergens, such as peanuts. Stay away from these foods, too, especially if your allergy is severe.

EMERGENCY PLAN

Some people have mild allergic reactions, such as hives or an upset stomach. Other people have severe reactions. The most severe reaction is called anaphylaxis (aa-nuh-fuh-LAK-suhs). That's when a person has a lot of trouble breathing and passes out. It needs to be treated right away, or it could be deadly.

Make a plan for your allergic reactions. If your reactions are severe, your doctor might give you emergency medicine to carry with you. You can **inject** the medicine into your body like a shot.

TELL ME MORE

If you have mild allergic reactions, you can take medicine to stop histamine in a pill. This medicine is called antihistamine.

If you have to use your emergency allergy shot, you still need to go to the hospital after. Doctors want to make sure your reaction doesn't come back.

YOU ARE NOT ALONE!

When you have an allergy, you might wonder why it's happening to you and why other people can eat the foods that you can't. You aren't alone. Nearly 3 million kids in the United States have food allergies.

It's important to learn about your allergy. Ask your doctor which foods are safe and which you should avoid. Keep eating healthy, even when it seems hard. Don't be **embarrassed** to speak up about your allergy. It may keep you from having an allergic reaction and can even save your life.

GLOSSARY

allergen: Something that causes an allergic reaction.

challenging: Requiring extra effort.

embarrassed: Feeling shame or uneasiness.

histamine: A chemical in a person's body that makes them have an allergic reaction.

inject: To force something into the body using a needle.

lactose intolerant: Having to do with an illness that makes it hard for the body to break down lactose, which is a sugar found in milk and dairy foods.

protection: Something that keeps someone safe.

react: Doing something because of something else.

severe: Very strong.

INDEX

WEBSITES

Due to the changing nature of Internet links, PowerKids Press has developed an online list of websites related to the subject of this book. This site is updated regularly. Please use this link to access the list: www.powerkidslinks.com/ltai/food